1,000,000 Books

are available to read at

Forgotten Books

www.ForgottenBooks.com

Read online
Download PDF
Purchase in print

ISBN 978-1-330-50928-9
PIBN 10071519

This book is a reproduction of an important historical work. Forgotten Books uses state-of-the-art technology to digitally reconstruct the work, preserving the original format whilst repairing imperfections present in the aged copy. In rare cases, an imperfection in the original, such as a blemish or missing page, may be replicated in our edition. We do, however, repair the vast majority of imperfections successfully; any imperfections that remain are intentionally left to preserve the state of such historical works.

Forgotten Books is a registered trademark of FB &c Ltd.
Copyright © 2018 FB &c Ltd.
FB &c Ltd, Dalton House, 60 Windsor Avenue, London, SW19 2RR.
Company number 08720141. Registered in England and Wales.

For support please visit www.forgottenbooks.com

1 MONTH OF FREE READING

at

www.ForgottenBooks.com

By purchasing this book you are eligible for one month membership to ForgottenBooks.com, giving you unlimited access to our entire collection of over 1,000,000 titles via our web site and mobile apps.

To claim your free month visit: www.forgottenbooks.com/free71519

* Offer is valid for 45 days from date of purchase. Terms and conditions apply.

English
Français
Deutsche
Italiano
Español
Português

www.forgottenbooks.com

Mythology Photography **Fiction**
Fishing Christianity **Art** Cooking
Essays Buddhism Freemasonry
Medicine **Biology** Music **Ancient Egypt** Evolution Carpentry Physics
Dance Geology **Mathematics** Fitness
Shakespeare **Folklore** Yoga Marketing
Confidence Immortality Biographies
Poetry **Psychology** Witchcraft
Electronics Chemistry History **Law**
Accounting **Philosophy** Anthropology
Alchemy Drama Quantum Mechanics
Atheism Sexual Health **Ancient History**
Entrepreneurship Languages Sport
Paleontology Needlework Islam
Metaphysics Investment Archaeology
Parenting Statistics Criminology
Motivational

MEMOIRS

OF THE

EARLY LIFE

OF

BENJAMIN WEST.

BOSTON—L. C. BOWLES.
NO. 124 WASHINGTON STREET.

George Henry Wilherle

Drawn by Beranger.   J. Russell Pxt   Engraved by F. Gallaudet

THE YOUNG ARTIST.

Published by L. C. Bowles, Boston

THE PROGRESS OF GENIUS,

OR

AUTHENTIC MEMOIRS OF THE EARLY LIFE

OF

BENJAMIN WEST, ESQ.

President of the Royal Academy, London.

COMPILED FROM MATERIALS FURNISHED BY HIMSELF
BY JOHN GALT.

Abridged for the use of young Persons, By a Lady.

BOSTON:
LEONARD C. BOWLES,
M DCCC XXXI.

Gift of Miss Amy C. Witherle
2 July 1930

DISTRICT OF MASSACHUSETTS, *to wit*:
District Clerk's Office.

BE IT REMEMBERED, that on the twelfth day of November, A. D. 1830, in the fifty-fifth year of the independence of the United States of America, Leonard C. Bowles of the said District, has deposited in this office the title of a book, the right whereof he claims as proprietor, in the words following, *to wit*

The Progress of Genius, or Authentic Memoir of the Early Life of Benjamin West, Esq, Resident of the Royal Academy, London. Compiled from materials furnished by himself, by John Galt. Abridged for the use of young persons. By a Lady.

In conformity to the Act of the Congress of the United States entitled 'An Act for the encouragement of learning, by securing the copies of Maps, Charts and Books, to the Authors and Proprietors of such copies, during the times therein mentioned;' and also to an Act entitled 'An Act suplementary to an Act, entitled, an Act for the encouragement of learning, by securing the copies of Maps, Charts and Books to the Authors and Proprietors of such copies during the times therein mentioned; and extending the benefits thereof the arts of designing, engraving, and eeching historical and other prints.'

JNO. W. DAVIS, *Clerk of the District of Massachusetts.*

THE INSPIRED BOY.

A boy!—yet in his eye you trace
   The watchfulness of graven years,
And tales are in that serious face
   Of feelings early steeped in tears;
     And in that tranquil gaze
  There lingers many a thought unsaid—
    Shadows of other days,
Whose hours with shapes of beauty came and fled.

  And sometimes it is even so—
    The spirit ripens in the germ,
  The new sealed fountains overflow,
    The bright wings tremble in the morn.
  The soul detects some passing token,
    Some emblem of a brighter world,
  And with its shell of clay unbroken,
    Its shining pinions are unfurled,
     And, like a blessed dream,
  Phantoms, apparelled from the sky,
    Athwart its vision stream—
As if the light of heaven had touched its gifted eye.

iv

'T is strange how childhood's simple words
   Interpret nature's mystic book—
How it will listen to the birds,
   And ponder on the running brook,
     As if its spirit fed.
And strange that we remember not,
Who fill its eye and weave its lot,
    How lightly it were led
Back to the home which it has scarce forgot.

THE LIFE OF WEST.

Benjamin West, the subject of the following memoir, was the youngest son of John West and Sarah Pearson, and was born near Springfield, in Chester county, in the State of Pennsylvania, on the 10th of October, 1738. About the year 1667 the family from which Mr West descended, embraced the tenets of the quakers, and in 1699 they emigrated from England to America.

Thomas Pearson, the maternal grandfather of the artist, was the confidential friend of William Penn, and the same person to whom that venerable legislator said on landing in America, 'Providence has brought us safely hither; thou hast been the companion of my perils, what wilt thou that I should call this place?' Mr Pearson replied, that 'since he had honored him so far as to desire him to give that part of the country a name, he would, in remembrance of his native city, call it Chester.'

The exact spot where these patriarchs of the new world first landed, is still pointed out with reverence by the inhabitants.

Mr Pearson built a house and formed a plantation in the neighborhood which he called Springfield, in consequence of discovering a large spring of water in the first field cleared for cultivation; and it was near this spot that Benjamin West was born. When the West family emigrated, John, the father of Benjamin, was left to complete his education at the great school of the Quakers at Uxbridge and did not join his relations in America till the year 1714. Soon after his arrival he married Sarah Pearson, the mother of the artist and of the worth and piety of his character we have a remarkable proof in the following transactions, which, perhaps, reflect more real glory on his family than the achievements of all his heroic ancestors. As a part of the marriage portion of Mrs West, he received a negro slave, whose diligence and fidelity very soon obtained his full confidence.

Being engaged in trade, he had occasion to make a voyage to the West Indies, and left this young black to superintend the plantation, or farm, in his absence. During his residence in Barbadoes, his feelings were greatly hurt, and his principles shocked, by the cruelties to which he saw the negroes subjected in that island, and the debasing effects were forcibly contrasted in his mind, with the morals and intelligence of his own slave. Conversing on this subject with Dr Gammon, who was then at the head of the society of friends in Barbadoes, the Doctor convinced him that it was contrary to the laws of God and nature that any man should retain his fellow creatures in slavery. This conviction could not rest long inactive in a character formed like that of Mr West. On his return to America he gave the negro his freedom. Not satisfied with doing good himself, he endeavored to make others follow his example, and in a short time his example had such an effect on his neighbors, that after some public discussion on the subject, it was resolved by a considerable majority *that it was the duty of Christians to give freedom to their slaves.* Their example was followed by the Quakers in the township of Goshen, in Chester county, and finally, about the year 1753, the same question was moved in the annual general assembly at Philadelphia, when it was established as one of the tenets of the Quakers, that no person could remain a member of their society who held a human creature in slavery thus making a great public sacrifice of their own interests, purely from moral and religious principle. They were not satisfied with the benevolent work of restoring their natural rights to the unfortunate negroes, but the society of Friends went further, and established schools for the education of their children ; and some of the first characters among themselves volunteered to superintend the course of instruction.

The first six years of Benjamin's life passed away in calm uniformity ; leaving only the placid remembrance of enjoyment. In the month of June, 1745, one of his sisters, who had been married some time before, and who had a daughter, came with her infant to spend a few days at her father's. When the child was asleep in the cradle, Mrs West invited her daughter to gather flowers in the garden, and committed the infant to the care of Benjamin, during their absence; giving him a fan to flap away the flies from molesting his little charge. After some time the child happened to smile in its sleep, and its beauty attracted his attention. He looked at it with a pleasure he had never before experienced, and observing some paper on a table, together with pens and red and black ink, he seized them with agitation, and endeavored to delineate a portrait; although at this period he had never seen an engraving or a picture, and was only in the seventh year of his age.

Hearing the approach of his mother and sister, he endeavored to conceal what he had been doing; but the old lady observing his confusion, inquired what he was about, and requested him to show her the paper. He obeyed, intreating her not to be angry. Mrs West, after looking some time at the drawing with evident pleasure, said to her daughter, 'I declare he has made a likeness of little Sally,' and kissed him with much fondness and satisfaction. This encouraged him to say, that if it would give her pleasure, he would make pictures of the flowers, which she held in her hand, for the instinct of his genius was now awakened, and he felt that he could imitate the forms of those things which pleased his sight.

The drawing was shown by Mrs West to her husband, who was delighted with this early indication of talent in his son. From the first emigration, in 1681, the colony of Quakers had continued to thrive with a rapidity unknown to any other European settlements. America had been chosen by their ancestors, as an asylum in which they might enjoy that affectionate intercourse, which their tenets enjoined, free from the military influence, and political jealousies of England. At the birth of Benjamin West the colony had obtained great wealth, and the population was increasing rapidly. It was blest in the maxim upon which it had been fonned by William Penn, and the effects of his beneficence was felt throughout the settlement. In the houses of the principal families, unlimited hospitality formed a part of their regular economy. It was the custom among those, who resided near the highways, after supper, and the last religious exercise of the evening, to make a large fire in the hall, and to set out a table with refreshments for such travellers as might have occasion to pass during the night; and when the families assembled in the morning, they seldom found that their tables had been unvisited. This was particularly the care at Springfield. Poverty was never heard of in the land.

William Penn, and many of his friends traced their lineage to the ancient and noble families of England. In their desendants the pride of ancestry was so tempered with the meekness of their religious tenets, that it gave a sort of patriarchal dignity to their benevolence. The neighboring Indians mingled safe and harmless among the friends; and in the annual visits, which they were in the practice of paying to the plantations, they raised their huts in the fields and orchards without asking leave, nor were they ever molested. When the great founder of the state of Pennsylvania marked out the site of Philadelphia in the woods, he allotted a piece of ground for a public library. It was his opinion that the few hours of relaxation, which the first settlers enjoyed, could not be better improved than in reading good and serious books. It was the design of the Quakers to make mankind wiser and better, but they were unfriendly to the cultivation of taste, and no works of imagination were admitted into their library. The fine arts were likewise uncultivated among them, so that in the whole christian world, no spot was apparently so unlikely to produce a painter as Pennsylvania. It might, indeed, be supposed that a youth, reared in the midst of boundless forests, tremendous water falls and mountains, whose summits were inaccessible ' to the lightest foot and wildest wing,' was in the most favorable situation to imbibe a strong love either of poetry or painting. That beautiful scenery, though it charms the taste, refined and alive to its influence, *will not create* or *inspire the original talent* for poetry, painting, or any other of of the fine arts.

Of all the nations of Europe the Swiss are the least poetical, and yet the scenery of no other country seems so well calculated as that of Switzerland to awaken the imagination; and Shakspeare, the greatest of all modern poets, was brought up in one of the least picturesque districts of England.

Soon after the occurrence of the incident we have related, the young artist was sent to a school in the neighborhood. During his hours of leisure he was permitted to draw with pen and ink; for it did not occur to any of the family to provide him with better materials.

In the course of the summer a party of Indians came to pay their annual visits to Springfield, and being amused with the sketches of birds and flowers which Benjamin showed them, they taught him to prepare the red and yellow colors with which they painted their ornaments.

To these his brother added blue by giving him a piece of indigo, so that he was thus put in possession of the three primary colors.

The Indians also taught him to be an expert archer, and he was sometimes in the practice of shooting birds for models, when he thought that their plumage would look well in a picture.

His drawings at length attracted the attention of the neighbors; and some of them happening to regret that the artist had no pencils, he inquired what kind of things these were, and they were described to him as small brushes made of camel's hair fastened in a quill. As there were, however no camels in America, he could not think of any substitute, till he happened to cast his eyes on a black cat, the favorite of his father; when, in the tapering fur of her tail, he discovered the means of supplying what he wanted. He immediately armed himself with his mother's scissors and, laying hold of Grimalkin with all due caution, and a proper attention to her feelings, cut off the fur at the end of her tail, and with this made his first pencil. But the tail only furnished him with one, which did not last long, and he soon stood in need of a further supply. He then had recourse to the animal's back, his depredations upon which were so frequently repeated, that his father observed the altered appearance of his favorite, and lamented it, as the effect of disease. The artist with suitable marks of contrition, informed him of the true cause; and the old gentleman was so much amused with his ingenuity, that if he reproved him, it was certainly not in anger.

In the following year, Mr Pennington, a merchant of Philadelphia, who was related to the West family, came to pay a visit to Benjamin's father. This gentleman was also a quaker, and although very strict in his notions, was a man of pleasant temper and indulgent disposition. He noticed the drawings of birds and flowers round the room, unusual ornaments in the house of a quaker; and heard with surprise they were the work of his little cousin. He did not pretend to be a good judge of painting, but he thought them wonderful productions for a boy only entering on his eighth year, and being told with what poor materials little Benjamin had been furnished, he promised to send him a box of paints and pencils from the city. On his return home he fulfilled his engagement, and at the bottom of the box placed several pieces of canvas prepared for the painter, and six beautiful engravings.

The arrival of the box was an era in the history of the painter and his art. It was received with feelings of delight which cannot be described. He opened it and in the colors, the oils and the pencils, found all his wants supplied, even beyond his utmost conception. But who can tell the surprise with which he beheld the engravings; he who had never seen any picture but his own draw ings, nor knew that such an art as the engraver's existed! He sat over the box with admiring eyes; his mind was in a flutter of joy,—and he could not refrain from constantly touching the different articles to ascertain if they were real.

At night he placed the box on a chair near his bed, and as often as he forgot his prize, in sleep, he started suddenly and stretched out his hand to satisfy himself that the possession of such a treasure was not merely a pleasing dream. He rose at the dawn of day, and carried the box to a room in the garret, where he spread a canvas, prepared a pallet, and immediately began to imitate the figures in the engravings. Enchanted by his employment, he forgot the school hours, and joined the family at dinner without mentioning the manner in which his forenoon had been passed.

In the afternoon he again repaired to his study in the garret, and for several successive days he thus withdrew and devoted himself to painting. The schoolmaster, observing his absence, sent to ask the cause of it. Mrs West recollected that she had seen Benjamin going up stairs every morning, and suspecting that the box occasioned his neglect of the school, went to the garret and found him employed on the picture. Her anger was appeased by the sight of his performance, and changed to a very different feeling. He had not *condescended* to copy a single engraving, but had selected the most striking features from a number, and by combining and arranging them with wonderful taste and accuracy, had composed a picture as complete in the arrangement of the several parts and coloring of the whole as the most skilful artist could have painted, under the direction of a finished master.

His mother kissed him with transports of affection, and assured him that she would not only intercede with his father to pardon him for having absented himself from school, but would go herself to the master, and beg that he might not be punished. This delightful kindness and approbation, thus bestowed, encouraged the young painter to greater efforts; but who will not regret that the mother's over anxious admiration would not suffer him to finish the picture, lest he should spoil what she thought was already perfect, even with half the canvas bare. Sixty seven years afterwards Mr West had the gratification of seeing this piece in the same room, with his sublime painting of 'Christ Rejected,' on which occasion he declared that there were inventive touches of art in his first juvenile essay, which with all the knowledge and experience he afterwards acquired, he had never been able to surpass.

In the course of a few days after the affair of the painting, Mr Pennington paid another visit to Mr West, and was so highly pleased with the effect of his present, and the promising talents of his young relative, that he intreated the old gentleman to allow Benjamin to accompany him for a few days to Philadelphia. This was cheerfully agreed to, and the artist felt himself almost as much delighted with the journey as with the box of colors. Every thing in the town filled him with astonishment; but the view of the shipping, which was entirely new, particularly attracted his eye, and interested his imagination. When the first emotion of his pleasure and wonder had subsided, he applied to Mr Pennington to procure him materials for painting. That gentleman was desirous of getting possession of the first picture, and had only resigned his claims, in consideration of the mother's feelings, and on being assured that the next picture should be painted purposely for him. The materials were procured, and the artist composed a landscape, which comprehended a picturesque view of a river, with vessels on the water, and cattle pasturing on the banks.

While he was engaged in this picture, an incident occurred which though trivial in itself, had so much influence, in giving a decided bent to his genius, that it ought not to be omitted.

Samuel Shoemaker, an intimate friend of Mr Pennington, and one of the principal merchants in Philadelphia, happened to meet in the street with one Williams, a painter, carrying home a picture. He was struck with the beauty of the painting, and inquired if it was intended for sale, and being told that it was already sold, he ordered another to be painted for himself. When the painting was finished, he requested Mr Williams to carry it to his friend's, Mr Pennington's house, in order that it might be shown to young West. He was so much astonished at the sight of it, and betrayed so much emotion and delight, that Mr William's observation was attracted toward him, no doubt with a good deal of interest and sympathy. He entered into conversation with him, and inquired if he had read any books, or the lives of great men. Young West told him that he had read the Bible, and was well acquainted with the history of Adam, Joseph, David, Solomon, and the other great and good men whose actions are recorded in the Holy Scriptures. Williams was much pleased with the simplicity of the answer; and it might have occurred to him that histories more interesting have never been written, or written so well. Turning to Mr Pennington, who was present, he asked if Benjamin was his son, advising him at the same time to indulge him in his present pursuits, assuring him that he was no common boy; he afterwards lent him the works of Fresnoy and Richardson on painting, and invited him to see his pictures and drawings. The effect which these books had on the imagination of West, finally decided his destination. He was allowed to carry them with him into the country; and his father and mother soon observed a great change in his style of conversation produced by his study of the books we have named—their effect on his mind, may be conceived of, by the following incident. Soon after the young artist had returned to Springfield, one of his school fellows, on a Saturday's half-holiday, engaged him to give up a party at trap-ball to ride with him one to the neighboring farms. At the time appointed the boy came, with the horse saddled. West inquired how he was to ride; 'Behind me,' said the boy; but Benjamin, full of the dignity of the profession to which he felt himself destined, answered that he would never ride behind any body. 'Oh! very well then,' said the good natured boy, 'you may take the saddle, and I will get up behind you.' Thus mounted they proceeded on their way; and the boy began to tell Benjamin that his father intended to send him to be an apprentice. 'In what business?' inquired West. 'A tailor,' answered the boy. 'Surely,' said West 'you will never follow that trade;' telling him at the same time that it was fit employment only for females. The boy was a shrewd sound headed lad and defended his father's choice very stoutly, saying that the person with whom he was to learn the business was much respected by all his neighbors. 'But what do you intend to be Benjamin?' West answered, that he should like to be a painter. 'A painter!' exclaimed the boy, 'what sort of a trade is a painter? I never heard of such a thing.' 'A painter,' said West, 'is a companion for kings and emperors.' 'Surely you are mad,' replied the boy, 'for there are no such people in America;' 'Very true,' answered Benjamin, 'but there are plenty in other parts of the world.' The other still more amazed, repeated in a tone of greater surprise, 'you are surely quite mad.' To this the young artist, still proud of his own choice, replied by asking him if he really intended to be a tailor. 'Most certainly,' answered the other. 'Then you may ride by yourself, for I will no longer keep your company,' said West, jumping from the horse, and immediately returned home.

The report of this incident, with the affair of the picture, which had occasioned his absence from school, and visit to Philadelphia, made a great impression on the boys in the neighborhood of Springfield. All their accustomed sports were neglected, and their play hours devoted to drawing with chalk and oker. Benjamin it must be confessed was the most expert among them, but he often afterwards declared, that, according to his recollection, many of his juvenile companions, evinced a degree of taste and skill in this exercise, that would have done no discredit to the students of any regular academy.

Not far from the residence of Mr West a cabinet-maker had a shop, in which Benjamin sometimes amused himself with the tools of the workmen. One day several large and beautiful boards of poplar tree were brought to it; and he happening to observe that they would answer very well for drawing on, the owner gave him two or three of them for the purpose, and he drew figures, and compositions on them with ink ,chalk and charcoal.

Mr Wayne, a gentleman of the neighborhood, having soon after occasion to call at his father's, noticed the boards in the room, and was so much pleased with the drawing, that he begged the young artist to allow him to take two or three of them home, which, as but little value was set on them, was thought no great favor, either by the painter or his father. Next day Mr Wayne called again, and after complimenting Benjamin on his taste and proficiency, gave him a dollar for each of the boards, which he had taken away, and intended to preserve.

Doctor Jonathan Morris, another neighbor, soon after also made him a present of a few dollars to buy materials to paint with. These were the first public patrons of the artist.

About twelve months after the visit to Philadelphia, Mr Flower, one of the justices of the County of Chester, who possessed some taste for painting, requested Mr West to allow Benjamin to spend a few weeks at his house. A short time before, this gentleman had lost an amiable wife, to whom he was most tenderly attached; and he resolved to show his respect to her memory by devoting his attention exclusively to the improvement of his children; for this purpose he had sent to England for a governess qualified to undertake the education of his daughters, and he had the good fortune to obtain a lady eminently fitted for the trust. She arrived only a few days before the young artist—but she soon discovered the bent of Benjamin's genius, and the strength and determination of his mind. Finding him unacquainted with any other books than the Bible, and the works of Richardson and Fresnoy, she frequently invited him to set with her pupils, and during the intervals of their tasks, she read to him the most striking passages from ancient history and poetry. It was from this intelligent woman that he heard, for the first time, of the Greeks and Romans, and the impression which the history of those illustrious nations made on his mind, was answerable to her expectations.

Among the acquaintance of Mr Flower was a Mr Ross, a lawyer in the town of Lancaster, a place at that time remarkable for its wealth, and which had the reputation of possessing the best and most intelligent society in America, those who knew how to distinguish real genius, from mere mechanical art. It was exactly in such a place that such a youth as Benjamin West was likely to meet with that flattering attention, which is the greatest stimulous to juvenile talent. The wife of Mr Ross was greatly admired for her beauty, and she had several children who were so remarkable in this respect as to be the objects of general notice. One day when Mr Flower was dining with them he advised his friend to have their portraits taken, and mentioned that they would be excellent subjects for young West. They accordingly obtained permission of Mr West's for the little artist to go to Lancaster, for the purpose of taking the likeness of Mrs Ross and her family—so great was his success in this undertaking that it was with difficulty he could answer the demand for portraits; among those who applied to him was a person named William Henry, an able mechanic, who had acquired a handsome fortune by his profession of a gunsmith. On examining the young artist's performance, he told him that, if *he* could paint as well he would not waste his time on portraits, but would devote his time and talents to some historical piece, and mentioned the death of Socrates as a good subject. The painter knew nothing of the history of the philosopher; and upon confessing his ignorance, Mr Henry, took a volume of Plutarch's lives and read to him the account given by that writer of this affecting story. The description produced a great effect on the imagination of young West, and induced him to make a drawing, which Mr Henry approved and requested him to paint. West said he should be happy to undertake the task, but having only painted faces, and men clothed, he should be unable to do justice to the slave, who presented the poison to Socrates, and which he thought ought to be naked. Henry had among his workmen a very handsome young man, and without hesitating a moment he sent for him into the room. On his entrance he pointed him out to West, and said 'there is your model.' The appearance of the young man, whose arms and breast were naked, convinced the artist that he had only to look into nature for the best of models. When the death of Socrates was finished, it attracted much attention, and led to his fortunate acquaintance with Dr Smith, the provost of the college at Philadelphia. After seeing the picture and conversing with the artist, he offered to undertake to make him, to a certain degree, acquainted with classical literature; while at the same time he would give him such a sketch of the taste and spirit of antiquity as would have all the effect of the regular education requisite for a painter.

Old Mr West readily consented that his son should go for some time to Philadelphia to take advantage of the provost's instructions, and accordingly after returning home for a few days, Benjamin went to the capital, and resided at the house of his brother-in-law, Mr Clarkson, a gentleman who had been educated at Leyden, and was much respected for the intelligence of his conversation and the propriety of his manners.

The plan of study which provost Smith had formed for his pupil was extremely judicious. He regarded him as destined to be a painter; and on this account did not impose upon him those grammatical exercises of language, which are usually required from the young student of the classics, but directed his attention to those incidents which were likely to interest his fancy and furnish him at some future time subjects for the easel. In the midst of this course of education the artist happened to be taken ill of a slight fever, and when it had subsided, he was in so weak a state as to be obliged to keep his bed, and to have the room darkened. In this situation he remained several days, with no other light than what was admitted by the cracks in the window shutters, which had the usual effect of expanding the pupils of his eyes to such a degree, that he could distinctly see every object in the room, which to others appeared in perfect obscurity. While he was thus lying in bed, he observed the shadowy form of a white cow enter at one side of the roof, and walking over the bed, gradually vanish at the other. This appearance surprised him not a little, and he feared that his disease had deranged his mind, which his sister also suspected, when he related to her what he had seen. She went immediately and informed her husband, who accompanied her back to the chamber; and as they were standing near the bed West repeated the story; declaring, at the same moment, that he saw several little pigs running along the roof. This confirmed their fears, that he was delirious, and they sent for a physician. But the doctor could discover no symptoms of fever, the pulse was regular, the skin moist and cool, the thirst abated, and everything about the patient favorable to his recovery. Still the painter persisted in his story, and assured them that he then saw the figures of several of their mutual friends passing on the roof over his bed; and that he even saw fowls pecking, and the very stones of the street. All this time his friends could discern nothing of all he described, their eyes being unaccustomed to the gloom of the chamber, and the learned physician himself began to suspect that his patient was really delirious, and prescribing a composing mixture, which the painter submitted to swallow, took his leave, requesting Mrs Clarkson and her husband to come away and not disturb the painter. After they had all left him, curiosity overcame the effect of the medicine, and the artist got up, determined to find out the cause of this strange appearance. In a short time he discovered a knot-hole in one of the window shutters, and upon placing his hand over it, the visionary paintings on the roof disappeared. He then began to think there must be some simple natural cause for what he had seen; and having found out the way in which it acted, he called his sister and her husband into the room and explained it to them. When able to go down stairs Mr Clarkson gave him permission to cut a horizontal hole in the shutter in order to obtain, on the wall, a representation of the buildings on the other side of the street. The effect was as he expected, but, to his astonishment, the objects appeared inverted, and every one who passed, to be walking on his head. He did not then understand how this might be remedied, but on his return soon after to his father's, he had a box made with a hole in one of the sides, and adverting to the reflective power of the mirror, he contrived, without ever having heard of the instrument, to invent a Camera, which he found of great use to him, as the means of studying the picturesque appearance of nature, and he hailed the discovery as a revelation to promote his improvement in the art of painting.

In this favorable state of things he attained his 16th year, when his father became anxious to see him settled in some established business, for though he had been indulgent to the genius of his son, the old gentleman was sensible that the profession of a painter was not only precarious, but regarded unfavorably by the religious society of which he was a member ; and he was anxious on his son's account, and on his own, to avoid those observations to which he was exposed by the freedom he had hitherto granted to the predilections of Benjamin. He therefore consulted several of his neighbors on the subject; and a meeting of the society of Friends in the vicinity was called, to consider publicly, what ought to be the destiny of his son.

The assembly met in the meeting-house near Springfield, and after much debate, approaching to altercation, a man of the name of John Williamson rose and delivered a very extraordinary speech upon the subject. He was much respected by all present, for the purity and integrity of his life, and enjoyed great influence on account of his superior natural wisdom, and an astonishing gift of eloquence, as a public preacher among the Friends.

He pointed to old Mr West and his wife, and expatiated on the blameless reputation they had so long maintained, and merited so well.

'They have had,' said he, 'ten children whom they have carefully brought up in the fear of God and in the christian religion, and the youth whose lot in life we are now convened to consider, is Benjamin, their youngest child. It is known to you all that God is pleased, from time to time, to bestow upon some men extraordinary gifts of mind, and you need not be told by how wonderful an inspiration their son has been led to cultivate the art of painting. It is true that our tenets deny the utility of that art to mankind. But God has bestowed on this youth a genius for the art, and can we believe that Omniscience bestows his gifts but for great purposes? What God has given, who shall dare to throw away? Let us not estimate almighty wisdom by our notions; let us not presume to arraign his judgment by our ignorance, but in the evident propensity of the young man, be assured that we see an impulse of the divine hand operating towards some high and beneficent end.'

The effect of this argument, and the lofty manner in which it was delivered, induced the assembly to agree that the young artist should follow the bent of his genius; and a private meeting of the Friends was appointed to be holden at his father's house, at which the youth himself was requested to be present, in order to receive the assent and blessing of the society.

On the day of meeting, the great room was put in order, and a numerous company of both sexes assembled. Benjamin was placed by his father, and the men and women took their respective forms on each side. After sitting some time in silence, one of the women arose and addressed the meeting, on the wisdom of God and the various occasions in which he selected from among his creatures the agents of his goodness. When she had concluded, John Williamson also arose; and in a speech of most impressive oratory, resumed the topic, which had been the subject of his former address. At the conclusion of this address, the women rose and kissed the young artist, and the men one by one, laid their hands on his head, and prayed that the Lord might verify in his life the value of the gift which had induced them, in despite of their religious tenets, to allow him to cultivate the faculties of his genius. The history of no other individual affords an incident so extraordinary. It may be added that a more beautiful instance of liberality is not to be found in the records of any religious society. There is something at once simple and venerable in the humility with which they regarded their own peculiar principles, contrasted with the sublime view they appeared to take of the wisdom and providence of the Deity. It would be impossible to convey any idea of the sentiments and feelings with which it affected the youth who was the object of its exercise. It inspired him with a lofty desire to attain eminence in his profession, nor did he forget in the honors which he afterwards received from all polished nations, that he was authorized by his friends and his religion, to cultivate the art by which he obtained such distinctions, not for his own sake, but as an instrument chosen by Providence to desseminate the arts of peace, to draw the ties of affection closer, and diffuse over a wider extent of community the interests and blessings of paternal love.

When it was determined among the Friends that Benjamin West should be allowed to cultivate the art of painting, he went to Lancaster, but was hastily recalled by a severe domestic misfortune. His mother was siezed by a dangerous illness, and being conscious that she could not live long, she requested that he might be sent for home.

Benjamin hastily obeyed the summons, but before he reached the house, her strength was exhausted, and she was only able to express by her countenance the satisfaction with which she saw him approach the bed, before she expired.

Her funeral, and the distress which the event occasioned to her family, by all of whom she was most tenderly beloved, detained the young artist some time at his father's. About the end of August 1756, however, he took his final departure, and went to Philadelphia.

But before proceeding with the narrative of his professional career, it is necessary to refer to the public transactions of that period, by which his sensibility was powerfully excited.

After the destruction of Gen. Braddock's army, the Pennsylvanians being alarmed at the defenceless state in which they were placed by that calamity, they resolved to raise a militia force; and Mr Wayne, who has been already mentioned as a friend to West, was appointed colonel of the regiment raised in Chester county. This defensive measure was painfully felt by the peaceful quakers, as it indicated an alteration in their harmless manners and habits, so averse to war and strife. West, among others, went to view the first muster of the troops under the command of Col. Wayne, and the sight of the men in arms, their purpose and array, warmed his lively imagination with military ardor. With a son of Colonel Wayne, a boy of his own age, with whom he had become acquainted, he procured a gun, and determined also to be a soldier. Young Wayne was regularly drilled; and he in turn exercised

West, who being alert and active, soon obtained 'a decided superiority. But what different destinies awaited them! West attained, in the exercise of a peaceful art, an enviable reputation, and Wayne who was then his inferior in military skill became afterwards an illustrious commander, and partook, with Washington, of the glory of having established the Independence of America. West soon after his drilling under young Wayne, visited Lancaster; and the boys of that town having formed themselves into a little company, made choice of him for a commander. Among those who caught the military spirit was his brother Samuel, who possessed a bold and enterprising disposition. He was six years older than Benjamin, and was appointed Captain in Colonel Wayne's army, under the command of General Forbes, who was sent to repair the disasters which had happened to the unfortunate Braddock; and to search for the relics of his army. As the European soldiers were not so well qualified to explore the forests, Capt. West was appointed, with his company of American sharp-shooters to assist in the execution of this duty, and a party of Indian warriors were requested to conduct him to the places where the bones of the slain were likely to be found. In this solemn and affecting duty, several officers belonging to the British regiment accompanied the detachment, and with them major sir Peter Halket, who had lost his father and brother in the fatal destruction of the army. It might have been thought a hopeless task that he should have been able to select their remains from the common relics of the other soldiers; but he was induced to think otherwise, as one of the Indian warriors assured him that he had seen an officer fall near a remarkable tree, which he thought he could still discover, telling him at the same time, that the incident was impressed on his memory by observing a young soldier, who in running to the officer's assistance, was also shot dead on reaching the spot, and fell across the other's body.

The major had a painful conviction in his own mind that the two officers were his father and brother, and, indeed; it was chiefly owing to his anxiety on the subject, that this pious expedition was undertaken. Capt. West and his companions proceeded through the woods, and along the banks of the river towards the scene of battle. The Iudians regarded the expedition as a religious service, and guided the troops with awe, and in profound silence. The soldiers were affected with sentiments not less serious, and as they explored the bewildering mazes of those vast forests, their hearts were often melted with inexpressible sorrow, for they frequently found skeletons lying across the trunks of fallen trees, a mournful proof to their imaginations that the men who sat there had perished of hunger, in vainly attempting to find their way to the plantations. Sometimes their feelings were raised to the utmost pitch of horror, by the sight of sculls and bones scattered on the ground—a certain indication that the bodies had been devoured by wild beasts; and in other places they saw the blackness of ashes amidst the relics —the tremendous evidence of atrocious Indian rites.

At length they reached a turn of the river, not far from the principal scene of destruction, and the Indian, who remembered the death of the two officers, stopped; the detachment also halted.

He then looked round in search of some object, which might recal distinctly his recollection of the ground, and suddenly darted into the wood. The soldiers rested their arms without speaking. A shrill cry was soon after heard, and the other guides made signs to the troops to follow them to the spot from which it came. In the course of a short time they reached the Indian warrior, who by his cry had announced to his companions that he had found the place where he was posted on the day of battle. As the troops approached, he pointed to the tree under which the officers had fallen. Capt. West halted his men round the spot, and with Sir Peter Halket, and the other officers, formed a circle, while the Indians removed the leaves which thickly covered the ground. The skeletons were found, as the Indian expected, lying across each other. The officers having looked at them some time, the major said, that as his father had an artificial tooth, he thought he might be able to ascertain if they were indeed his bones and those of his brother. 'The Indians were therefore ordered to remove the skeleton of the youth, and to bring to view that of the old officer. This was immediately done, and after a short examination Major Halket exclaimed, 'It is my father,' and fell back into the arms of his companions. The pioneers then dug a grave, and the bones were laid in it together, a highland plaid was laid over them, and they were interred with the customary honors.— The gloom of the vast forest, the naked and simple Indians supporting the skeletons, the grief of the son oh recognizing the relics of his father, the subdued melancholy of the spectators, and the picturesque garb of the Pennsylvanian sharp shooters, were ever after present to the imagination of West as one of the most affecting occurrences under which the service was ever performed.

On his return to Philadelphia, he again resided with Mr Clarkson, his brother-in-law, and provost Smith, in the evenings, continued to direct his studies. While his leisure hours were thus profitably employed, his reputation as a portrait painter was rapidly extended, and he looked forward to the time, when he might be enabled, by the fruits of his own industry, to visit the great scenes of the fine arts in Europe, and the care with which he treasured the money that he received for his portraits, was rewarded even at the time with the assurance of realising his expectations. The prices which he first fixed for his portraits, were two guineas and a half a head, and five guineas for a half length. While he was thus employed on portraits a gentleman of the name of Cox called on him to agree for a likeness of his daughter, and a portrait which West had made of his friend and patron, Dr Smith, attracted his attention. It appeared to him to evince such a taste for historical painting, that instead of then determining anything respecting his daughter's portrait, he gave an order for an historical picture, allowing the artist himself to choose the subject. He made choice of the trial of Susannah; for in the course of reading the Bible to his mother some time before, he had been led to think the trial of Susannah was a fine subject. He made his canvass about the size of a half length portrait, on which he introduced no fewer than forty figures. It is not known what has become of this painting; but in point of composition, Mr. West was of opinion that the Trial of Susannah was superior to the Death of Socrates.

But although West found himself constantly employed in Philadelphia, he was sensible that he could not expect to increase his prices, if he continued constantly in the same place; he was also very desirous to see more of the world and mankind; and, beyond all, he was profoundly sensible, by this time, that he could not hope to attain eminence in his profession, without inspecting the great masterpieces of art in Europe, and comparing them with his own works, in order to ascertain the extent of his powers. Accordingly, impressed with these considerations, he frugally treasured the earnings of his pencil, that he might undertake, in the first place, a professional journey from Philadelphia. When he found that the state of his funds enabled him to undertake the journey, he went to New York. He found society there much less intelligent in matters of taste and knowledge than at Philadelphia. The population of New York was formed of adventurers from all parts of Europe, who had come thither for the express purpose of making money, and therefore wholly devoted to mercantile pursuits. Although West found in that city much employment in taking likenesses, destined to be sent across the Atlantic to relations and friends, he met with but few in whom he found any disposition and taste congenial to his own; and the eleven months which he passed there contributed less to the improvement of his mind than might have been expected from a city so flourishing.

In the year 1759, the harvest in Italy fell far short of the usual crops, and two merchants of Leghorn wrote to their correspondent, Mr Allen, at Philadelphia, to send them a cargo of wheat and flour. Provost Smith hearing that Mr Allen intended sending out his son commander of the vessel, immediately waited on the old gentleman, and begged him to allow West to accompany him, which he cheerfully agreed to, and the provost immediately wrote to his pupil at New York on the subject. In the mean time, West had heard there was a vessel at Philadelphia loading for Italy, and had expressed to Mr William Kelly, a merchant, who was then sitting to him for his portrait, a strong desire to avail himself of this opportunity to visit the fountain head of the arts. Before this period, he had raised his terms for a half length portrait to ten guineas, by which he acquired a sum of money sufficient to defray the expenses of a short excursion to Italy. When he had finished Mr Kelly's portrait, that gentleman, in paying him, requested that he would take charge of a letter to his agents in Philadelphia, and deliver it to them himself, on his return to that city. It stated to the concern to which it was addressed, that it would be delivered by an ingenious young gentleman, who intended to visit Rome for the purpose of studying the fine arts, and ordered them to pay him fifty guineas as a present from him towards furnishing his stores for the voyage; an instance of delicate munificence which cannot be too highly applauded. The artist having embarked with young Allen had a speedy and pleasant passage to Gibraltar, where in consequence of the war then raging, the ship stopped for convoy. After touching at several ports on the coast of Spain, the ship arrived safely at Leghorn, where mercantile affairs detained Mr Allen some time, and West being impatient to proceed to Rome, bade him adieu. Before his departure from Philadelphia, he had paid into the hands of old Mr Allen the money which he thought would be requisite for his expenses in Italy, and had received from him a letter of credit on Messrs Jackson & Rutherford. When they were made acquainted with the object of his voyage, and heard his history, they showed him a great deal of attention, and presented him with letters to Cardinal Albani, and several of the most distinguished characters for learning and taste in Rome; and as he was unacquainted with French or Italian, they recommended him to the care of a French courier, who had occasion to pass that way.

When the travellers had reached the last stage of their journey, while their horses were baiting, West walked on alone. It was a beautiful morning; the air was perfectly placid, not a speck of vapor in the sky, and a profound tranquillity seemed diffused over the landscape. The appearance of nature was calculated to lighten and elevate the spirits; but the general silence and nakedness of the scene touched the feelings with solemnity approaching to awe. He looked for a spot to rest on, that he might contemplate at leisure a scene at once so noble and so interesting; and near a pile of ruins fringed and trellissed with ivy, he saw a stone that appeared to be a part of a column. On going towards it, be perceived that it was a mile-stone, and that he was then only eight miles from the capital. It was on the 10th July, 1760, that he arrived at Rome. The French courier conducted him to a hotel, and having mentioned in the house that he was an American, and a quaker, come to study the fine arts, the circumstance seemed so extraordinary, that it reached the ears of Mr Robinson, afterwards Lord Grantham, who immediately felt an irresistible desire to see him; and who before he had time to dress or refresh himself, paid him a visit, and insisted that he should dine with him. In the course of dinner, that gentleman inquired what letters of introduction the artist had brought with him, on looking at them he observed that it was somewhat remarkable that the whole of them should be addressed to his most particular friends, adding that as he was engaged to meet them at a party in the evening, he expected West would accompany him. This attention and frankness was acknowledged and remembered by the artist, among those fortunate incidents which have rendered the recollection of his past life so pleasant as scarcely to leave a wish for any part of it to have been spent otherwise than it was. At the hour appointed, Mr Robinson conducted him to the house of Mr Crispigné, an English gentleman who had long resided at Rome, where the evening party was held. Among the distinguished persons whom Mr West found in the company, was the celebrated cardinal Albani. His eminence, although quite blind, had acquired, by the exquisite delicacy of his touch, and the combining powers of his mind, such a sense of ancient beauty that he excelled all virtuosi then in Rome.

Mr Robinson conducted the artist to the inner apartment, where the cardinal was sitting, and said, 'I have the honor to present a young American, who has a letter of introduction to your eminence, and who has come to Italy for the purpose of studying the fine arts. The cardinal fancying that the American must be an Indian, exclaimed, 'Is he black or white?' and on being told that he was very fair, 'What, as fair as I am?' cried the cardinal still more surprised. This latter expression excited a good deal of mirth at the cardinal's expense, for his complexion was of the darkest Italian olive, and West's was uncommonly fair. The cardinal, after some other short questions, invited West to come near him, and running his hands over his features, attracted the attention of the company to the stranger, by the admiration he expressed at the form of his head. This occasioned inquiries respecting the youth; and the Italians concluding, that as he was an American, he must, of course, have been brought up as a savage, became curious to witness the effect which the works of art contained in the Belvidere and Vatican, would produce on him. The whole company, which consisted of the principal Roman nobility, and strangers of distinction then in Rome, were interested in the event; and it was arranged that on the following morning they should accompany Mr Robinson and his protegé to the palaces. At the hour appointed the company assembled; and a procession, consisting of upwards of thirty of the most magnificent equipages in the city, and filled with some of the most learned characters in Europe, conducted the young quaker to view the masterpieces of art. It was agreed that the statue of Apollo should be first submitted to his view, because it was the most perfect work among all the ornaments of Rome, and of course, the best calculated to produce that effect, which the company were anxious to witness. The statue then stood in a case, enclosed with doors, which could be so opened as to disclose it at once to full view. West was placed in the situation where it was seen to the most advantage, and the spectators arranged themselves on each side. When the keeper threw open the doors, the artist felt himself surprised by a sudden recollection, and without being aware of the force of what he said, exclaimed, ' My God, how like it is to a young Mohawk warrior!' The Italians, observing his surprise, and hearing but not understanding the exclamation, requested Mr Robinson to translate to them what he said; and they were excessively mortified to find that the god of their idolatry was compared to a savage. Mr Robinson mentioned to West their disappointment, and asked him to give some explanation, by telling them what sort of people the Mohawk Indians were. He described to them their education, their dexterity with the bow and arrow; the admirable elasticity of their limbs; and how much their active life expands the chest, while the quick breathing of their speed in the chase, dilates the nostrils with that apparent consciousness of vigor which is so nobly depicted in the Apollo. 'I have seen them often,' added he, 'standing in that very attitude, and pursuing, with an intense eye, the arrow which they had just discharged from the bow.' This explanation did not lose, by Mr Robinson's translation, and the Italians were delighted, saying that a better criticism had rarely been pronounced on the merits of the statue.

The view of the other great works of the art did not awaken the same vivid feelings. In the evening, after visiting the palaces, Mr Robinson carried Mr West to see a grand religious ceremony in one of the churches. Before this, he had been acquainted only with the simple worship of the quakers. The pomp of the Roman Catholic ceremonies was as much beyond his comprehension, as the overpowering excellence of the music surpassed his utmost expectations. Undoubtedly he possessed a keen relish for the spectacles and amusements of Rome, arising from the simplicity of his education and habits. But neither the Apollo, the Vatican, nor the pomp of the catholic religion, excited his feelings to so great a degree, as the spectacle which presented itself to his view around the portico of the church. Bred in the universal prosperity of Pennsylvania, where the benevolent were employed in acts of hospitality and mutual kindness, he had never witnessed any spectacle of beggary, nor had he ever heard the name of God uttered to urge an entreaty for alms. Here, however all the lazars and the wretched of Rome were collected 'together, hundreds of young and old in that extreme squalor, nakedness and disease, were seen on all sides, and their importunities and cries, 'for the love of God, and the mercy of Christ!' to relieve them, thrilled in his ears, and smote upon his heart to such a degree, that his joints became as it were loosened, and his legs scarcely able to support him. As they returned from the church, a woman somewhat advanced in life, and of a better appearance than most of the beggars, followed them; and Mr West gave her a small piece of copper money, the first Roman coin which he had received in change, and the value of which was unknown to him. Shortly afterwards they were joined by some of the Italians, whom they had seen in the morning, and while they were conversing together, he felt some one pull his coat, and turned round. It was the poor woman to whom he had given the piece of copper money. She held out in her hand several smaller pieces; as he did not understand her language, he concluded that she was chiding him for having given her such a trifle, and colored deeply with the idea. His English friend observing his confusion, inquired what he had given her, and he answered that he did not know, but it was a piece of money, he had received in change. Robinson after a short conversation with the beggar, told Mr West that she had asked him for a farthing, 'But as you gave her a twopenny piece,' said he, 'she has brought you the change.' This instance of humble honesty, contrasted with the awful mass of misery with which it was united, gave him a favorable idea of the latent sentiments of the Italians.

At this time Mengs (a famous Italian artist) was in the height of his popularity, and West was introduced to him at the cardinal's villa. He was as much struck as any other person, with the extraordinary circumstance of an American coming to study the fine arts; and begged that Mr West would show him a specimen of his drawing. In returning home our artist mentioned to Mr Robinson that as he had never learned to draw, he could not produce any sketch like those made by the other students; but that he could paint a little, and if Mr Robinson would take the trouble to sit, he would execute his portrait to show to Mengs. The proposal was readily acceded to, and it was also agreed, that except to two of their most intimate acquaintances, the undertaking should be kept a profound secret. When the picture was finished, it did him great credit, but before showing it to Mengs, it was resolved that the taste and judgment of the public, with respect to its merits, should be ascertained.

Mr Crespigné, one of the two friends entrusted with the secret, lived as a Roman gentleman, and twice a year gave a grand assembly at his house, to which all the nobility and strangers of distinction, in Rome, were invited. It was agreed that the portrait should be exhibited at one of his parties, which happened to take place soon after it was finished. A suitable frame being provided, the painting was hung up in one of the rooms. The first guests who arrived were amateurs and artists, and as they knew that Robinson was sitting to Mengs for his portrait, it was at once thought to be that picture, and they agreed that they had never seen any painting of that artist so well colored. As the guests assembled the portrait became more and more the subject of attention, and Mr West sat behind on a sofa, equally agitated and delighted by their observations, which Mr Robinson reported to him from time to time. Mr Crespigné seizing the proper moment in their conversation to produce the effect intended, said 'The picture is not painted by Mengs.' 'By whom then?' vociferated every voice, ' for there is no other painter now in Rome capable of executing anything so good.' 'By that young gentleman there,' said Mr Crespigné, turning to West. At once all eyes were bent towards him, and the Italians, in their way, ran and embraced him. Thus did the best judges at once, by this picture, acknowledge him as only second in his art to the first painter then in Rome. Mengs himself, on seeing the picture, expressed his opinion in terms that did honor to his liberality, and gave the artist an advice which he never forgot, nor remembered without gratitude.

He told him the portrait showed, that he had no occasion to learn to paint at Rome—' You have already, sir,' said he, ' the mechanical part of your art: what I would therefore recommend to you, is to see and examine everything deserving of attention here, and after making a few drawings of about half a dozen of the best statues, go to Florence, and observe what has been done by art in the collections there, then proceed to Bologna and study the works of Caracca. afterwards visit Parma, and examine, attentively, the pictures of Coregio; and then go to Venice and view the productions of the great masters there. When you have made this tour, come back to Rome, and paint an historical composition, to be exhibited to the Roman public; and the opinion which will then be formed of your talents, should determine the line of our profession you ought to follow.' This judicious advice, West found accord so well with his own reflections and principles, that he resolved to follow it with care and attention. But the thought of being in Rome, and the constant excitement arising from extraordinary and interesting objects, so affected his mind, accustomed to the sober and uniform habits of the quakers, that sleep deserted his pillow, and he became ill, and constantly feverish. The public took an interest in his situation. A consultation of the best physicians in Rome was held on his case, the result of which was a formal communication to Mr Robinson, that his friend must immediately quit the capital, and seek relief in quiet and retirement. Accordingly on the 20th of August he returned to Leghorn.

Messrs Jackson and Rutherford, received him into their own house, and treated him with a degree of kindness and hospitality that merits for them the honor of being considered among the number of his early patrons.

His mind being thus relieved from the restless delight which he felt at Rome, together with the bracing effect of sea-bathing, he was soon in a condition to resume his study in the Capital. But the same overpowering excitement of his feelings and imagination, soon produced a relapse of his former disorder, and compelled him to return to Leghorn, where he was again speedily cured of his fever, but it left him with a painful affection in the ankle, that threatened the loss of the limb. An eminent surgeon, who had introduced many improvements in the treatment of diseased joints, was at this period resident in Florence, and Messrs Jackson and Rutherford wrote to Sir

Horace Mann, then British minister at the ducal court, to consult him relative to the case of Mr West: his answer induced them to advise the artist to go to Florence. After a painful period of eleven months confinement to his couch and chamber, he was perfectly and radically cured. A state of pain and disease is adverse to mental improvement; but there were intervals in which Mr West felt his anguish abate, and in which he was not only able to join in the conversation of the gentleman to whom he had been recommended, but was able, occasionally, to exercise his pencil. When he was so far recovered as to be able to take exercise, and to endure the fatigue of travelling, a circumstance happened which may be numbered among the many fortunate accidents of his professional career. Mr Mathews, the manager of the important commercial concerns of

Messrs Jackson and Rutherford was one of those singular men, very rarely met with in mercantile life, combining the highest degree of literary and elegant accomplishments, with the best talents for active business. Affairs connected with the business of the house, and a wish to see the principal cities of Italy, led Mr Mathews about the period of Mr West's recovery, to visit Florence, and it was agreed between them that they should together make the tour recommended by Mengs. In the mean time the good fortune of West was working to happy effects in another part of the world. The story of Mr Robinson's portrait had made so great a noise among the travellers in Italy, that Messrs Jackson and Rutherford, in sending back the ship to Philadelphia mentioned it in their letters to Mr Allen. It happened that on the very day this letter reached

Mr Allen, Mr Hamilton, then governor of Pennsylvania, and the principal members of the government, along with the most considerable citizens of Philadelphia were dining with him. After dinner Mr Allen read the letter to the company, and mentioned the amount of the sum of money which West had paid into his hands, at the period of his departure from America, adding that it must be pretty far reduced. But, said he with warmth, 'I regard this young man as an honor to the country, and as he is the first that America has sent to cultivate the fine arts, he shall not be frustrated in his studies, for I have resolved to write to my correspondents at Leghorn, to give him from myself, whatever money he may require.' Mr Hamilton felt the force of this generous declaration, and said with equal animation, 'I think exactly as you do, sir, but you shall not have all the honor of it, to yourself, and, therefore, I beg that you will consider me as joining you in the responsibility of the credit.' The consequence of this was, that upon West's going, previously to leaving Florence, to take a small sum of about ten pounds from the bankers, a letter was brought in while he was waiting for his money, and the gentleman who opened it, said to him, ' that the contents of the letter would probably afford him unexpected pleasure, as it instructed him to give him unlimited credit.' A more splendid instance of liberality is not to be found even in the records of Florence.

From Florence the artist proceeded to Bologna, and having stayed some time there, carefully inspecting every work of celebrity to which he could obtain access, he went on to Venice, visiting in his route all the objects which Mengs had recommended to his attention.

Having completed his tour to the most celebrated repositories of art in Italy, and enriched his mind and improved his taste by the perusal, rather than the imitation of their best pieces, he returned to Rome, and applied himself to a minute and assiduous study of the great ornaments of that capital. In the meantime West was carefully furnishing his mind by an attentive study of the costume of antiquity, and the beauties of the great works of modern genius. In doing this, be regarded Rome only as a university, in which he should graduate; and, preparatory to taking his degree among the students, he painted a picture of Cimon and Iphigenia, and, likewise another of Angelica and Madoro. The applause which they received justified the opinion which Mengs had so early expressed of his talent, and certainly answered every object for which they were composed. He was honored in consequence, with the marks of academical approbation, usually bestowed on fortunate artists. He then proposed to return to America, with a view to cultivate in his native country that profession, in which he had already acquired so much celebrity. At this juncture he received a letter from his father, advising him to *go home* for a short time before coming to America; for the mother country was at that period still regarded as the home of her American offspring. The advice of his father was in unison with his own wishes. He could hardly have resolved on quiting 'Italy more opportunely, for Dr Patonne, a Scottish gentleman, of considerable learning, and some taste in painting, was then returning homeward, and waiting at that time in Rome, until he should be able to meet with a companion. It was therefore agreed that West should be introduced to him; and it was soon after arranged that the doctor should proceed to Florence, while the artist went to take leave of his friends at Leghorn, to express to them his gratitude for their constant and extraordinary kindness, which he estimated too highly to allow him to think of leaving Italy, without performing this pleasing and honorable pilgrimage. It was also agreed between him and his companion, that the doctor should stop a short time at Parma, until West should have completed a copy of the St Jerome of Corregio, which he had begun during his visit to that city with Mr Mathews.

During their stay at Parma, the academy elected him a member, an honor which the academies of Florence and Bologna had previously conferred on Mr West; and it was mentioned to the prince that a young American had made a copy of the St Jerome of Corregio, in a style of excellence such as the oldest academicians had not witnessed. The prince expressed a wish to see this extraordinary artist, particularly when he heard that he was from Pennsylvania and a quaker. Mr West was accordingly informed that a visit from him would be acceptable at court; and it was arranged that he should be introduced to his highness by the chief minister. Mr West thought that, in a matter of this kind, he should regulate his behaviour by what he understood to be the practice in the court of London; and accordingly, to the astonishment of all the courtiers, he kept his hat on during the audience. This however, instead of offending the prince, was observed with evident pleasure, and made his reception more particular and distinguished; for his highness had heard of the peculiar simplicity of the quakers, and of the singularly christian conduct and principles of William Penn.

From Parma he proceeded to Genoa, and thence to Turin; they then proceeded to France, but remained no longer in Paris than was necessary to inspect the principal works of the French artists, and the royal collections. Mr West, however, continued long enough to be satisfied, that the true feeling for the fine arts did not exist among the French to that degree he had observed in Italy. He next proceeded to England, where we must reluctantly leave him—as this memoir was compiled from materials furnished by himself, and was intended to embrace only that period of his life, previous to his visiting England. The professional life of Mr West constitutes an important part of an historical work, in which the matter of this volume could not have been well introduced. Mr West, in relating the circumstances by which he was led to understand, without the aid of an instructer, those rules of art, which it is the object of schools and academies to teach and diffuse, has conferred a greater benefit on young artists than he could possibly have done by the most ingenious and eloquent lectures on the theory of his profession; and it was necessary that the narrative should appear in his own life time, in order that the truth of the incidents related might not rest on the authority of any biographer.